I Knew He Had A Plan

Elder Latausher L. Fletcher

Copyright © 2019 by Latausher L. Fletcher

All rights reserved. In accordance with the U.S. Copyright Act of 1976, the scanning, uploading, and electronic sharing of any part of this book without the permission of the publisher is unlawful piracy and theft of the author's intellectual property. If you would like to use material from the book, prior written permission must be obtained by contacting the publisher at info@entegritypublishing.com.
Thank you for your support of the author's rights.

Entegrity Choice Publishing
PO Box 453
Powder Springs, GA 30127
info@entegritypublishing.com
www.entegritypublishing.com
770.727.6517

Printed in the United States of America

The views expressed in this work are solely those of the author and do not necessarily reflect the views of the publisher, and the publisher hereby disclaims any responsibility for them.

Scriptures are quoted from the King James Version of the Bible unless otherwise noted.

The publisher is not responsible for websites (or their content) that are not owned by the publisher.

Library of Congress Cataloging-in-Publication Data
ISBN 978-1-7330301-0-6
Library of Congress 2019941665

In Memoriam

*My beloved sister Vella R. Brook,
brother Rev. Darrion K. Fletcher,
my Pop Mr. John Huzzie, and
Reverend O. Weems.
Rest on, my Beloved, in Jesus's arms.
I will see you all in the morning.*

*To the loves of my life:
gone but never forgotten, my parents,
Mr. James R. and
Mrs. Mattie Kate Fletcher.*

Words of Encouragement

To encourage another child of God, as the Spirit leads, is easy to do. But to encourage a sister and friend, is even easier.

Elder Latausher Fletcher, your love for God causes you to take advantage of every good gift. Now that you have committed another gift (this book) to the Lord, even the sky is not a limit for you. Your life's journey has been challenging sometimes, but the word of God promises that it will all work out for your good. It was not all good, but it is surely working out for good.

I thank you for standing strong despite what you went through, and for your tremendous testimony. So many people will be blessed and believe that they too, can get through tough times, because of what you have shared.

We are blessed if we can be a blessing to others, and you are truly a blessing to the Body of Christ. I am grateful that our paths crossed. You have made a positive, permanent impression on my life.

Keep on serving the Lord. He has His hands on you, for His glory.

Because of Him,
Rev. Bettye Holland Williams

Acknowledgements

To my blood line: Twallace, Della, James, Sheila, and Marcus.

To my heart beat: Eddie (Darnell), my first born; Laquandra, my first-born daughter; the two that God blessed me with, Jaqueze, and Shuntanay.

To my sunshine, Godmother Mrs. Dorothy Willis; my spiritual mother, Dr. Ernestine Weems; Elder Farr-Cannon; and my close friend, Pastor Bettye H. Williams.

To my first love: my church family at Simpson Road Baptist Church.

To my church family whom I love from the depths of my heart: Changing A Generation Full Gospel Baptist Church and my Beloved Pastors, Bishop Paul S. Morton, and Co-Pastor, Dr. Debra B. Morton.

To everyone that is reading this book: may God bless you real good.

Contents

Words of Encouragement............ vii

Foreword........................xiii

Introduction...................... xv

Chapter 1
   How It Began.................. 1

Chapter 2
   You Know My Way............. 9

Chapter 3
   He Hides Me in His Arms...... 15

Chapter 4
   God Is Always With Us........ 23

Chapter 5
   The Lord Is My Keeper 33

Chapter 6
   The Devil Tried to Destroy
   My Life..................... 41

Contents

Chapter 7
    I Know Who I Am............. 47

Chapter 8
    Know Your Haters 59

Chapter 9
    A New Heart 69

Chapter 10
    Conclusion................... 77

About the Author.................. 83

Foreword

Psalm 90:9 tells us that we spend our years as a tale that is told. Thanks be to God for Latausher's inspiration to "show and tell" what great things the Lord has brought to pass in her life.

For sure, we have a gracious and awesome God — One that initiates, forgives, accepts, and redeems. Through the years, I have watched this writer grow, mature, and develop. There were always indications that God had a special plan and purpose for her life. She is happy, ambitious, excited, zealous; always endearing, with bright eyes and a charming smile; always at the height of class and style. That's Latausher! She is a God-fearing young woman. "Charm is deceitful, and beauty is vain, but a woman that fears the Lord is to be praised." (Proverbs 31:10-31) As in Proverbs 1:7, it is the fear of the Lord that is "the beginning of wisdom."

As we read her words of encouragement, let us resolve to give our best to the Master. May our hearts be open to hear the poignant cries of a world that is hungry for the living bread.

"Let us be steadfast, unmovable, always abounding in the work of the Lord, lifting the Savior up for them to see, for we know that our labor is not in vain in the Lord."

(1 Corinthians 15:58)

**To God be the Glory!
Dr. Ernestine J. Weems**

Introduction

I always knew God had a plan for my life, but I always wondered how God was going to do it. Growing up, struggling with a learning disability led me to sexual immorality. That is when I began to doubt His plans. In my mind, I just could not see how God could use me in His Kingdom. I remember one of the first scriptures I learned in Sunday School:

"For God so loved the world, that He gave His only begotten Son, that whosoever believeth in Him should not perish, but have everlasting life."
John 3:16 KJV

All I have to do is believe in Him, and I will have eternal life here on earth. He came so that I would have a good life. God has demonstrated His love for me over and over again. The devil tried many times to take me out. Devil, I call notice on you; it won't work. When I was in my mother's womb, the devil knew God was getting ready to birth this bold, black woman, who was going to stand on His Word, no matter what. Even if I had to stand alone.

God has given me the power to tear Satan's kingdom down! God knew He could trust me with His business. Now, we know we cannot trust everybody with our business. That is how God is. You have to be tested and ordained for God to trust you with His business. He has to see if we are fit for the journey. It means you have to give up some things and some people. You may have to cry sometimes. You may have to walk alone. Just know, it is for God's glory. As you read this book, keep in mind that when man says no, God says yes. When you don't have much and don't know what to do, God can still use you for His glory. God has a plan for you. You

Introduction

will find His plan when you seek Him. He knows your path. He is waiting on you.

Moses thought that he was not good enough. Let me share this with you: we live in a world where people will make you think that you are not good enough or smart enough. I am here to tell you to put your trust in God. He knows what you can do. He knows how smart you are. He definitely knows what you have, because He is the only one who supplies your needs. I challenge you to look to Jesus, God's only son. He is sitting on the right hand of the Father interceding on your behalf.

In my growing up years, I had some challenges. I am so grateful that I know a GOD that sits high and looks down low on me. I recall walking the campus of Oral Roberts University in Tulsa, Oklahoma, talking with God. That is when my whole life shifted. I have never been the same. God has given me the ability to preach His Word. I am thirsty for His Word.

In 2004, I started a women's Bible

study fellowship, where women came together to study God's Word and apply it to their daily lives. We wanted to become better women and serve with unity and not with jealousy. In 2018, God called the women's fellowship back together with a brand-new vision. Now it is a place to discuss real life, real talk, real pain, and real issues. I believe that we should put it out there and get some real results.

On June 14, 2008, I graduated from B.J. Holland Institute of Ministry and was licensed in the ministry, and ordained on November 1, 2009. I was ordained by the Full Gospel Baptist Church Fellowship International College of Elders, on July 16, 2015. I am on the road to greatness. God has honored my sacrifice, and I got my glory back. Hallelujah!

1
How It Began

I recall my mother saying that it was very hot the day I was born. On her way to the hospital to deliver me, she held her head out the window to collect air in her lungs. The heat was unbearable as she made her way down the road in "the hearse," (which is what they called ambulances back in that day).

She also told me that, when I was born, I was the most beautiful baby girl, with a head full of hair. Well, I don't know what happened to all those luscious locks she used to speak of. Both of my parents, Mr. James and Mrs. Mattie Kate Fletcher, were loving and honest parents who had seven other wonderful kids. I grew up with my brothers and sisters, as well as a dog. There were ten of us, plus one dog in our home.

 My parents always spoke to us about Jesus. We had one of those big Bibles in the house that we read. Sometimes our parents would ask us to find a scripture. We would have Bible study at home, and my parents would be our teachers. My father was an intelligent man. He was protective and powerful, always putting goodness in our ears and teaching us right from wrong.

 My mother was one of the best cooks I knew. She could clean a home until it was spotless. She was a collector of antique glasses, which was always unique to me. She loved to have the cabinet full of glasses. Believe it or not, even with eight children, we ate and drank out of glassware. She did not believe in paper cups and plates. We only used paper products on holidays or when company came over to our house for dinner. I got my love of glassware, to this day, from my mom's influence.

People would be in disbelief when they came over and saw the house spotless, even with eight kids in the house. My mom would get asked how she did it, and her response would always be, "I teach my children." My father instilled responsibility in us at an early age. When I say he was a father that didn't play, I mean he did not play! He would always say that his eight kids would not grow up irresponsible. But, at the same time, he was the most loving father anyone could have. He made life a breeze for us. He always told us he loved us and made sure we knew he cared about us.

We had a lot of gatherings in our home. My father didn't really like us to be around other kids, especially if their parents didn't raise them the way we were raised. He believed a half-raised child would do anything. We were taught to act right, do right, and believe in God. If my parents were away, my oldest sister, Twallace, was in charge. If she wasn't there, then the next oldest would be in charge, my sisters Della and Vella, who were twins. Guess who was next in line when they weren't there. Me! And that was an accomplishment back in our days.

I was the kind of child who always did what she wanted to do and didn't care who was in charge. There was one thing I was scared of, and that was a whooping. I'll never forget how Dad talked to us about how we shouldn't do something that will hurt us in the end, which meant we would get a whooping. He'd also talk to us about how to love one another, no matter the circumstances. Until this day, we have never turned on one another, because that was what was taught to us as brothers and sisters. If you mess with one of us, you mess with all of us.

That's exactly how it was when we went to school. All of us were a year apart from each other. My two brothers were the same age for one month. Then, one of my brothers and I were the same age for two months. My mother gave us all our first, middle, and last names. Wow! She had a brilliant mind and was very creative! One thing I can say, my parents were obviously in love and couldn't keep their hands off each other.

    Everybody knew the Fletchers. We could not go to the movies or house parties with just our friends. We had to all go together or with our cousins. Dad would say, "Y'all go together, and y'all better come back together." Don't get it twisted, thinking the Fletchers had it all together; we didn't. Trust me, we had our bad days and still do. No family is perfect. Sometimes, it seems like peace left the house as soon as a dish wasn't clean or the floor wasn't swept. Our parents would say, "God don't dwell in an unclean place." I believed that Jesus could not come to our house if it wasn't clean. I didn't know that wasn't true until I studied the Word for myself.

Matthew 21:13 says, *"My temple will be called a house of prayer, but you are making it a hideout for thieving."* God was talking about His temple and our hearts. God couldn't come into our hearts unless we allowed Him to clean it out, so we had to show love to one another. That was a lesson to learn while we were young. We had our good and our bad days, though. We always had food to eat, a place to lay our heads, and clothes on our backs. It might not have been the fanciest way of life, but we had all we needed.

With ten people in our house, my mom would cook a lot of vegetables sometimes with no meat. I didn't really care for the beans and peas. That is why, until this day, I love me some chicken, hot dogs, and steak. I eat shrimp, bacon, and pork chops once every blue moon, but I try to stay away. I also learned growing up, that family is important to God. Genesis 15:5 says, *"He brought him forth abroad, and said, Look now toward heaven, and tell the stars, if thou be able to number them: and He said unto him, So shall thy seed be."* I am writing to let you know that God has a plan for you, your family, your enemies, and everyone. We are a chosen generation. This is what I have learned about my family.

We didn't get to choose our family; God chose them for us. We might have come from the same seed, but it doesn't entitle us to have the same personality. All of us are different, and anyone can tell the difference. We don't always flow the same way, but one thing I can't take away from the Fletchers is that we all look alike. The Fletcher DNA strand is strong. Because we are family, we'll never stop loving one another. Just keeping each other prayerful and uplifted is going to keep us strong. If anything needs to be fixed, let God put it together. He will do it.

Growing up with my family, taught me to live with no regrets, and to not try to change a thing about what life lessons were taught. If I had to live it all over again, I would. My prayer every night is, "Lord, please don't change anything." I thank God for my parents implanting their seed in us. Let them live on forever. Family matters to God. Family matters to me. We all love God and were taught to serve Him. My parents taught this to us when we were young. God told Moses in Deuteronomy 6:7, *"And thou shalt teach them diligently unto thy children, and shalt talk of them when thou sittest in thine house, and when thou walkest by the way, and when thou liest down, and when thou risest up."* My parents taught us how to honor family and have respect for one another.

2
You Know My Way

"Thou compassest my path and my lying down, and art acquainted with all my ways." Psalm 139:3

When you grow up with so many siblings, there will always be a problem child. Guess who that problem child just so happened to be. Me. I never drank or did drugs, so that was never a problem, but my problem was sexual immorality, which triumphed in my life. It was a spirit that seemed to be worse than anything. Matthew 15:19 says, *"For out of the heart proceed evil thoughts, murders, adulteries, fornications, thefts, false witness, blasphemies:*

These are the things which defile a man …"

It's sad to say, I started having sex when I was in high school. And back then, that was a "no, no". You'd get killed by your parents, or at least by mine. Once I started, I got out of control. I started missing school and cutting classes. I'd go over to my children's dad's house or hang out over at friends' houses whose parents weren't home. I'd ride the bus downtown, and walk around, just being crazy and doing my own thing. Remember when I said my dad was no joke? Well, just because we were in high school didn't mean we wouldn't get a whooping.

As time passed, I got so bad, I was cutting class two or three times a week, just to go over to my children's dad's house. I was having sex, staying the night, and simply not being who I knew I was. Eventually, my dad even told him that if I came over to his house again, my dad would kill him. So, he got really scared and left me alone. At that point, my father was fed up and gave me two options. I either had to stop skipping school, actually attend school, and do what I could with my work or I had to leave home. I had to obey, because I had nowhere to go and I knew nothing about the street life.

I recollect walking from the bus stop, knowing I was going to get a whooping when I got home. I then heard a voice in my head saying, "It's time to do right, Tasha. I love you." I looked around, believing someone was talking to me from behind, but there was no one there. It reminded me so much of Saul on the road to Damascus. I knew something about what Saul heard, because we both grew up in the church. I wasn't persecuting anybody but myself. However, God told Ananias this about Saul, in Acts 9:15: *"But the Lord said unto him, Go thy way: for he is a chosen vessel unto me, to bear my name before the Gentiles, and kings, and the children of Israel:"* At that moment, I knew something was going on with me. When I got home, my father wasn't there. I went into my room and cried.

I cried all night, because something was going on inside me. I didn't understand what it was, until about twenty-five years later. People of God, understand, while we are on this road of life, sometimes we get sidetracked or fall off the path. We start trying to do our own thing, but when God has a plan for our life, we can run, but we can't hide. He found me walking down Pinehurst Street. He will definitely find you. God found Saul on the road to Damascus. He found Moses at Horeb (Exodus 3:1). He found Jonah in the belly of a fish (Jonah 1:17). God knows our way. It was later on in life, that I really began to do God's will. Now, I don't always have it together, and I don't always do it right, but I do thank God every day, that I've done and I know more right than wrong.

God knew my path of learning His Word. I thank the great and late Reverend O. Weems for planting seed at Simpson

Road Baptist Church. Thank God for him and his spiritual belief. He was a powerful man who taught my family the meaning of love and life. Now, I am at Changing A Generation Full Gospel Baptist Church, under the leadership of Bishop Paul S. Morton and Dr. Debra B Morton. I'd like to thank them for watering the seed to cause growth and development.

Thank you, Jesus, for saving me. God picked me up and turned my life around. He knew my way. Keep in mind: the devil is always looking for someone he can devour. *"And the Lord said unto Satan, Whence comest Thou? Then Satan answered the Lord, and said, From going to and fro in the earth, and from walking up and down in it."* Job 1:7

We already know that the Lord knows our way, but also, be aware that Satan knows our way as well.

3
He Hides Me in His Arms

*"Thou hast beset me behind and before, and laid thine hand upon me.
Such knowledge is too wonderful for me; it is high, I cannot attain unto it."*
Psalm 139:5-6

I knew, as a child, that my parents were praying for their children, especially me. I knew I was different from all my sisters and brothers. I knew God had me wrapped in His arms, and I believed He was always looking out for me. I know a lot of my behavior mentioned in chapter two, came from something that happened when I was six years old. When my father and mother were at work, the lady next door would baby sit us. When she was watching us, she would ask me to go to the store to buy her some cigarettes. Back then, you could just write a note with what you wanted and the store would give it to you.

The neighbor lady knew that my parents never let us go out of the house or the yard by ourselves. So, my baby sister and I, as well as the little boy next door went to the store. As we were on our way to the store, we took a shortcut through some apartments. We saw a man standing in his door, with his rod on. He asked us where we were going. Since I was the oldest, I answered, "To the store." He asked, "Can you bring me something back from the store?" I said, "Yes." He told me to come in and get the money, so I came into the living room. Then, he went into his room. He called me back to his room and told me to look down under his bed, and get the money. He claimed that it had dropped on the floor. I got down and looked under his bed. While I was down there, his rod hit the floor. I looked up, and he had no clothes on.

He picked me up and threw me on top of his bed and got on top of me. I started yelling and crying, until he got off of me. I got up and ran out the door of his bedroom, and out of his apartment. My baby sister and the little boy that was with us, started running with me. We ran all the way home. When we got there, we told the baby sitter what happened, and she called my parents.

First, my dad came home, and then my aunt came. My mother was coming in at the same time, and she called the police. My dad was running around the neighborhood, looking for someone he didn't even know. He had no way of knowing what the man even looked like. All I can hear is my lovely father saying, "I am going to kill him." I thank God that he did not find the man, because I could not imagine losing my dad to prison during my growing up years.

The police took my mother and I to

the hospital, for them to examine me. When we got back, I remember the police coming back to take my parents and I downtown for me to pick the man out of the line-up. I picked him out right when I walked in, and looked at him. I did not see him anymore, until we went to court. My dad was sitting in the courtroom, and the next thing I knew, my dad had jumped over the bench and table to get to the man. He yelled, "I am going to kill you!" If you ever saw the movie, "Time to Kill," you will understand how my daddy was, that day. The police took my dad downstairs to arrest him. They banned my dad from the courtroom until the case was over.

 I missed many days from school, because of going back and forth to court. I could not forget what happened. Every time I had to talk about it, I relived it all over again. My dad used to talk about how he wished he could have protected his family. One thing I can say: as long as my dad was living, I always felt safe.

I pray that God will bless me with a husband that I will feel safe with. But my God reminds me in Psalm 91:4, *"He shall cover thee with His feathers, and under His wings shalt thou trust: His truth shall be thy shield and buckler."* You see, I am safe in His arms.

My mother said the man went to Morris Brown College. His parents didn't have much money, so he did not stay on campus. I don't know where he ended up, but one thing I do know: he left this little girl, who was smart and bright, in a very dark world. That is when my learning disability started. Because I felt shut down all throughout my school years, I was just going through the motions.

Back then, they did not have help like they do now. My parents just became over-protective. We could not go over to anyone's house, except for my aunt's house, to spend the night. We could not go anywhere at all, unless all of us were together. Dad did not let anybody babysit us. He stayed at home. My dad's eyes were always on his family. All that was good, but it did not help this little girl. Nobody asked me how I felt.

That is why, now, I always ask people what is on their minds. I know that, if the mind is not stayed on the Word of God, it can have you living all kinds of ways and doing things that do not please God. Romans 1:28 says, *"And even as they did not like to retain God in their knowledge, God gave them over to a reprobate mind, to do those things which are not convenient."* Some people are doing things in their life, because no one asked them what is on their mind. Because, what happened to them, in the past, leads them to unrighteous sexual immorality (like me), or to murder, deceit, disobedience to parents, or so much more. But the Bible is teaching us, in Colossians 3:2, to *"set your affection on things above, not on things on the earth."* I am sorry for the ones who are not asked, what is on their mind, causing their life to turn out wrong. My parents did not get me counseling, but they gave me Jesus.

A year after that horrible event, we moved. One day, my mother went to the store down the street from the house. She looked down from the store and saw a church. Easter was coming soon. My mother always dressed us up every Easter. She told us to go there. We went. My oldest sister and I joined the church, about a month later, and got baptized. I was eight years old. I stayed there thirty-seven years, until God released me. However, that is still my first love, my home church - Simpson Road Baptist Church. That is where I first met Jesus, somewhere other than at home. That is where God renewed my mind. That is where the seed was planted. That is where I told the Lord that I will go wherever He sends me. The devil thought he had me, but God has always kept me in His arms. "I am safe in the arms of Jesus. I am safe on His gentle breast; shaded by His love, sweetly my soul shall rest."

4
God Is Always With Us

"Whither shall I go from Thy Spirit? or whither shall I flee from Thy Presence? If I ascend up into heaven, Thou art there: if I make my bed in hell, behold, Thou art there." Psalm 139:7-8

I let my mind go back to 1979. It was the year I turned 18, in July. I believed that I was grown up. I thought I could do what I wanted to do and go where I wanted to go. I was trying to do my own thing, but a father like mine must have thought I had lost my mind. I graduated in May, and in October, moved out of the house to live with my children's father. In 1983, I had my first child, my son, Eddie. I was young when I named my child Eddie after his father. You see, I was old school. Back then, you named your first son after their father. In 1987, I had my daughter, Laquandra, one of the most beautiful babies in the world.

My children had a good dad, but he had issues. However, Jesus still saves to the utmost. He did not want me to work. He just wanted me to stay at home, take care of the children, keep the house clean, and take care of him. As you know, I had grown up in the church, but he did not go to church. It wasn't long before I started staying home with him and missing church, until I heard that voice again say, "Do you love me more than these?" I couldn't see up ahead, but God could. My children's father got on drugs. Everything started to go downhill. I am here to challenge you: no matter what, NEVER - I mean NEVER - let anybody or anything, come between you and God! *But I knew that He had a plan.*

Here comes the devil again, trying to

get my focus. In 1993, they came out with a full-figured women's clothing line. Now I was not that big, but I had a nice body, and I have always liked to dress nice. When I was in school, there were eight siblings in school at the same time. My mom and dad could not buy all of us clothes at one time. So I was on early dismissal from school, to go to work, and was able to buy some of my own clothes. I got my love of dressing up from my father, and a desire to have my hair in place and make-up on, from my mother.

In the late '80s and early '90s, I started being in fashion shows at my church. Then I went to different places like private clubs: Bonner Brother Show, Catherine's Clothing for Women, or anywhere in Atlanta where there was a fashion show. Well, one day, I heard on the radio that they were looking for full figured women to be in a big fashion show. Some recruiters from Ashley Stewart would be there to recruit women to go big in the big city of

New York. I auditioned and was one of the ones picked. On top of that, they needed four ladies to make a commercial to advertise the fashion show, and I was one of the ones chosen to make the commercial. It only showed on cable. My mother did not have cable, so you know what she did? She got cable! Every time the Ad came on television and she saw me, she would just smile. I knew she was proud of me. My mother loved to see me walk into church, dressed from head to toe.

It seemed as if any time you turned on the television, they were playing the commercial. I would be out at the store or just hanging out, and people would say, "I know you from somewhere." I would always reply, "Church", because I did not hang out at the club. I would ask, "What church do you go to?" They would say, "None." Then I would probably say, "A commercial." They would say, "Yes." Their face would light up, as if they had just met someone popular and famous.

They would often comment, "You were sharp." I would say, "Thank you!"

The night of the fashion show came. The show was held in a five-star hotel in Atlanta. On that night, the Lord showed me favor. Believe me, at that time, I knew nothing about favor. I won the contest to go to New York. Eight other ladies and I, also won a trophy. When I got back to the dressing room, I had never seen so many jealous women in one room. I was so upset about how they made me feel. My emotions were all over the place. I left without saying goodbye to my family and friends, who had come out to support me. In my mind, I left those women in the dressing room, and said, "They all can go to hell." That is why I have a passion to break down jealous strongholds, and bring unity among women. I missed the opportunity to travel around the world, to become one of the best-dressed, full-figured models in the world.

There is one thing you need to know

about me. I have never cared about being popular or famous. I knew who I was when I was around popular people. I treat all people the same. Some people are doing too much, so I have to bring their mind back in. If I knew then what I know now, I would be that girl for real. *But God had a better plan.* I am here to tell you to never let anyone make you miss the opportunity God has for you. If the plan changes, make sure God does it, and not people with a jealous spirit. Some who hosted the fashion show called many days, until they gave up. One day, I was downtown shopping in Macy's, and I ran into the lady who discovered me. She looked at me and said, "Hello." She was glad and disappointed at the same time to see me, but she smiled and said, "You are still beautiful. What are you doing now?" She was still recruiting women for fashion shows. She was one of the most outstanding women in Atlanta. She attended Salem Baptist Church. She loved fashion. She could make anything without a pattern. She was a great woman of God. This was an interrupted plan, *but God had another plan.*

In 2008, I had another interrupted plan by God. I met this man. Correction, he met me. There goes my focus. He wanted me to marry him. He was a truck driver. I was not blind to love. He was thinking that this daughter of the King, Jesus Christ, was going to let him play me. He knew I was just called into ministry when I met him. He knew I was teaching and preaching God's Word. He had the nerve to get my focus off Jesus. He would say, "You're always in that church." If anyone knew me, they knew that was who I was. He only wanted God when he needed something, or wanted God to do something for him. God sees and knows everything. He doesn't miss a thing.

Well, what happened next is, I went to San Antonio, Texas, to get my CDL license to drive around the United States. All he wanted was worldly things and I was thinking of Kingdom vision. While I was away, he got on my nerves so bad, because he had the nerve to get smart with me. I was already in a strange place, feeling like I had turned my back on God. I just got licensed to preach. If you know me, you know that I don't allow people to talk to me any kind of way. I am not going for that. Jesus came to me like He was face-to-face with me, and said, "Do you love Me more than these?" John 21:15.

    I learned that, when we move too fast, God has to stop and ask us if we love Him. At that time, where I was worshiping, I was frustrated in my spirit. I don't play with God. That made it easy for me to leave. I was thinking about how God made a way for me, and how He is always taking care of me. I got up and went to my instructor, and told him I needed to go home. I started talking about my blood pressure. You cannot have high blood pressure and have a CDL. He took me back to the hotel to get my things. I had to ride Greyhound back home. It took me forty-eight hours to come back to Atlanta. I could not believe how long it took. Being on a such a long trip gave me the opportunity to interact with a lot of the people on the bus, even though I wanted to be alone. While on the bus, God had everybody telling me their problems. I was praying for people every time I looked around. God had me feed a whole family. I paid for a person's ticket that was hanging around at the bus stop, trying to get to California.

    When I got to Atlanta, I was drained. I definitely paid for stepping out of the will of God. I learned that, even if I make my bed in hell, He is there. I can tell you that Romans 8:35 is real. *"Who shall separate us from the love of Christ? Shall tribulation, or distress, or persecution, or famine, or nakedness, or peril, or sword?"* I am here to tell you, that I let nothing separate me from God's love. "At the cross is where I first saw the light and the burden of my heart rolled away, it was there by faith I received my sight, and now I am happy all the day."

5
The Lord Is My Keeper

"If I take the wings of the morning, and dwell in the uttermost parts of the sea; Even there shall thy hand lead me, and thy right hand shall hold me."
Psalm 139:9-10

People of God, when you belong to God, just know that God has got you. He will take care of you, no matter what you are going through. Jesus teaches us in John 10:29-30, *"My Father, which gave them me, is greater than all; and no man is able to pluck them out of my Father's hand. I and my Father are one."* You see, we have a powerful team.

I Knew He Had A Plan

We are covered by the blood of Jesus, even when we mess up. I have found myself in a lot of situations, trying to do my own things and leaving God out. In my younger days out of high school, a sexual immorality spirit just had me crazy. One day, my friend and I were heading out getting ready to "do the do." We were lying across the bed with our clothes on listening to music. My friend was smoking marijuana. I need to pause right here; I did not do drugs or smoke anything. My dad scared the hell out of me, so there was no way I was doing drugs or smoking. As we were laying on the bed, he rolled over and laid on top of me and began to blow smoke in my face. I began to feel funny. I started yelling, "Get off of me." He said, "What is wrong with you?" I said, "Move!" I got up and went to the door and opened it. He yelled, "What's wrong with you?" I said, "You're trying to kill me." He said, "Girl you are crazy; nobody is trying to kill you!" I started crying, and he began laughing at me. I told him that I did not see anything funny. When I was growing up, I was scared that I was going to die, or somebody was going to kill me. It is a terrible thing to grow up in fear.

    I ran for the door, and as soon as I got outside, I started running up the street thinking that I was losing my mind. My aunt stayed up the street, so I headed for her house. My friend jumped in his car and came after me. When he caught up with me, he told me to get into the car. I got inside the car and told him that I wanted to go home. On the way home, he stopped at the store to get me some milk. I have no idea why he wanted me to drink milk. I told him that I don't like milk. He told me to drink the milk; so I did.

    As my friend was turning on my street, in the distance, I could see my brothers and their friends sitting outside, talking and laughing. When I got out of the car, I told my brothers what had happened to me. My friend hurriedly pulled off to avoid my brothers, which was a wise move. My brothers did not play about their sisters. When I told them about the smoke I inhaled, they started laughing, but I became upset. They told me, "Girl, you just got a contact high from the smoke. You are going to be okay. Just keep drinking the milk." I learned later in life that people drink milk for poisoning. That encounter scared the hell out of me. If that incident had not scared me, I would probably be on drugs, but God had a plan. We live in a world where sex and drugs go hand in hand. But God is my Keeper.

"Keep me, O Lord, from the hands of the wicked; preserve me from the violent man; who have purposed to overthrow my goings." Psalm 140:4

The Bible teaches us in John 10:10, *"The thief cometh not, but for to steal, and to kill, and to destroy: I am come that they might have life, and that they might have it more abundantly."* God is omnipresent. He is present everywhere, so you can never be lost to His Spirit. This is good news to those who know and love God, because no matter what we do or where we go, we can never be far from God's comforting Presence.

When I was coming into the ministry to preach God's Word, it looked like everything that can go wrong went wrong with me. In 2010, I was beginning to have back problems. If you have problems with your back, then you know what I am talking about.

The Bible teaches us that a man who doesn't work, doesn't eat. I had to quit working, because I was in a car wreck. My car was totally lost. I could not get another car, because I did not have a job. I had to find another place to live. On top of all that, God gave me someone else's baby to raise. I said to God, "You're kidding me – right?" My children were grown and on their own. Well, you will hear this story again, because this is what turned my life around. I had to make the choice to change. Even with this unexpected life change, God always reminded me that He has me in His hands. No one can take you out of His hands. God kept me when I did not see my way. Without a doubt, He was making a way.

During my trials, I learned that people love to see you going through difficult times, so they can say we are not who we are in Jesus. But, let me share this with you: God sees our tears. He knows our heart. He feels our pain. And He knows our way. I challenge you to keep trusting in God until you die, no matter what. He is our Keeper. It might not look like it or feel like it, but He is there. If God brought me out, I know without a doubt, that He will bring you out. Get around some strong believers that don't look at what you have, but where you are going. Connect with others that have a heart for God and His people. Connect with someone that can give you a word and who lives on His Word.

I challenge you to try the spirit, by the Spirit, to see if it is of God. If not, get away from them. You have too much work to be doing for the Kingdom to be playing. They might not like you, but I can assure you that you will be okay. Trust me. You will. The song writer wrote, "There are some things I may not know. There are some places I cannot go. There is one thing that I am sure that God is real for I can feel Him in my soul." God is my Keeper.

6
The Devil Tried to Destroy My Life

"I say, surely the darkness shall cover me; even the night shall be light about me. Yea, the darkness hideth not from thee; but the night shineth as the day: the darkness and the light are both alike to thee." Psalm 139:11-12

I have had many dark days in my life. I vividly remember my godmother singing a song at church with the words, *"There is a bright side somewhere. Don't you stop till you find it. There is a bright side somewhere."* I did not think much of the words to this song until I got older. I came to understand that the bright side is *Jesus*. He can turn your darkness to light. The devil came at me many times, but God had His hand on me.

In 1981, the devil came to attack my mind, but I had a praying mother. My mother spent many nights with me, because the devil had me living in fear. In 1985, my body was attacked with welts and boils. I had a fever that was killing me. The doctor told my father it did not look good. I stayed in the hospital for more than a month. For almost two months, I was very sick. Please know that God has a plan for your life, and that no devil in hell can stop you. I recall looking out the hospital window thinking, "Lord, save my life. I am too young to die." Praise God! He had a plan and He healed me.

The devil kept trying to kill me. In 1986, I had a tubal pregnancy. Most women, at that time, did not survive this type of pregnancy. I was coming home on the train from work, and I passed out. I was able to give some kids next to me my mother's phone number, before I passed out. I remained unconscious, until the ambulance came to take me to the hospital. When I came to, I heard the doctor telling my father, once again, that it did not look good. They had to do emergency surgery.

My father signed the paper for the surgery. My mother was also there. My father did not play, when it came to his eight children. If anything went wrong with any of his children, he was there. Oh God, I miss him so much. I am crying now, just thinking about my parents. Well, I made it. The Lord brought me through. I know the devil is always trying to take me out.

When I was young, I did not know very much about God. *"I will extol You, o LORD, for You have lifted me up, and have not let my foes rejoice over me. O LORD my God, I cried out to You, and You healed me. O Lord, you brought my soul up from the grave; You have kept me alive, that I should not go down to the pit." Psalm 30:1-3 NKJV*

You see, the devil tried to take my life and make me lose my mind, but God had a plan. Even in my dark days, God was my light. In 2011, the devil tried again to attack my body. I had low back problems which slowed my journey down. I am glad to report that God is restoring me. The devil always seeks a chance to rejoice over our downfall.

For the past seven years, I have had many dark days. In 2011, I stopped working because of my back problems. My blood pressure was high, because I was always in pain. Let me tell you, God has a way of getting our attention. He used my back problems, no job, no car, and nowhere to live, as an avenue in which I ended up with someone else's baby. During this time, I stayed with family, and I don't think they really knew how I felt or what I was going through. They were used to me having it all together. It looked like I did, because every time I went down, I always had a way of coming back up.

If God is in something, it will happen in God's time. When I was down, people were laughing at me. Friends who I thought would stick with me until the end, walked away. Family members were talking about me. Even in my dark days, God said, "Hold your head up. It is not them. It's Me. No one can take anything from you. I am your Heavenly Father. I take care of you. You see, Latausher, I am getting you ready to speak to My people, and to tell them how to stand in dark days. They will have dark days."

Be careful who you laugh at and talk about. When God has people in a season of preparation, we win at the end. Isaiah 40:1-2 says, *"Comfort ye, comfort ye my people, saith your God. Speak ye comfortably to Jerusalem, and cry unto her, that her warfare is accomplished, that her iniquity is pardoned: for she hath received of the Lord's hand double for all her sins."* The Bible said Jerusalem still had one hundred years of trouble. God was telling Isaiah to speak tenderly to

His people. Sometimes, people will look at you, and they will try to make you feel bad, because you are still going through trouble. Don't forget this: there is a bright side somewhere. If it is not here on this earth, it will be with God on the other side. Now, that is joyful to think about!

    The seed of comfort may take root in the soil of adversity, when your life seems to be falling apart. Ask God to comfort you. You may not escape adversity, but you may find God's comfort as you face it. Sometimes, however, the only comfort we have, is in the knowledge that someday, we will be with God. Appreciate the comfort and encouragement in His Word, His Presence, and His people. And let the church say, "Amen." I am so glad that troubles don't last forever.

7
I Know Who I Am

"For thou hast possessed my reins: thou hast covered me in my mother's womb. I will praise thee; for I am fearfully and wonderfully made: marvellous are thy works; and that my soul knoweth right well." Psalm 139:13-14

Growing up, I always struggled with my learning disability. I found myself going through the school day, daydreaming a lot. When I came out of school, I was reading on a lower level. I was talked about. I was laughed at. Yes, that was me. Due to my learning disability, I used to hide or be alone, because I did not want people to know that I could not spell or read well. *God had a plan.* I did not like who I was. I had very low self-esteem. I began to pray about it. I started telling myself, "You are a smart, beautiful, and intelligent young lady."

I remember someone saying that all of the pretty girls are dumb, and all of the ugly girls are smart. I did not believe that, because I have some smart *and* pretty girls, who are family and friends. What I learned is when you have a learning disability, the world will overlook you. They will put you in a nobody class. But what really hurts, is that the church people will put you out as well. I thank GOD that He was saving me, and starting to build my confidence in Him.

I could have gone straight to college after graduating from high school to be a scientist, pilot, doctor or lawyer. I would have been one of the greatest lawyers, because I know how to win a case. However, He was saving me for Himself.

"The Spirit of the Lord God is upon me; because the Lord hath anointed me to preach good tidings unto the meek; he hath sent me to bind up the brokenhearted, to proclaim to the captives, and the opening of the prison to them that are bound." Isaiah 61:1

As I was growing up, I always had the ability to learn more and to expand my learning ability. God allowed me to come in contact with people who were very smart, educated and intelligent. In 1989, I started taking a reading class. With God's help, He restored my knowledge, and He broke the stronghold of the dark day that had me bound. My learning ability began to open up. Every time you saw me, I would be reading something. I recall reading the Bible, when I was younger in the hospital. I did not understand it then. I used to learn how to speak in church through repetition.

One thing I did not have to learn, was how to interpret God's Word. I knew it was a gift. I understood His Word, when I could not understand anything else. My beloved pastor, the late Rev. O Weems, knew I had a gift to interpret God's Word. He saw so much in me. I recall, one time, when my Pastor asked me to teach the adult Bible class, because he and his wife had to travel with the National Baptist Convention. They had positions as officers in the convention. Many times, when he had to be away, he asked me to teach. I told him that I don't know all that stuff in the Bible. When I would say that to him, I heard a voice come into my head and say, "Go with what you know. I am with you." I began to teach sometimes, even when he was not travelling.

 I was about thirty-three years old, when God opened this opportunity to teach. I always loved Bible class and Sunday school. There were a lot of smart people at my church. My oldest sister was smart. People started coming. Whatever reason they came, some knew they were smarter than me. It was not how smart I was; it was my anointing. It was not Rev. Weems; God just used him to put me in my rightful place. People were blessed. Lives were changed. I am a giver. Maybe I cannot give like I used to, but if you know me, you know I love blessing people, especially, those in need.

A jealous spirit from some began to surface. I did not run this time. They started saying, "She is trying to preach." Let me be clear, I was in a Baptist church, where women did not preach. Then they said that I was going out with the pastor. I knew that was a lie. He was just doing what God told him to do. The devil stirred up so much mess, until the pastor had to stop me from teaching. He did not want to lose anyone. I knew that, if he kept that door opened for me, every woman, thinking she had a call on her life, would be coming to him. Keep in mind, I did not go to him. The Lord trusted him with me. God does not trust everybody with me. I cried many days and nights. But God had a plan, and He was still pruning me.

I was a young lady- beautiful and attractive- and still dealing with that spirit of sexual immorality. Nevertheless, God still used me in the church. Oh, how I loved my church. I started teaching Sunday School. God allowed me to speak on Women's Day. I was always faithful to God's Word and to His people. In 1989, my Pastor came to me and asked me if I wanted to go to the Baptist Convention. It was held in New Orleans. I said yes. It was on a national level. I enjoyed myself. I was one of the youngest people that went. My church paid for everything. I stayed at the Doubletree Hotel on Canal Street, for a whole week. From that time on, I started going every year. I did not see the connection at the time. My pastor was over the late-night service. I became one of the delegates that traveled with the church to the convention. Well, you know what happened. Everybody started saying why

I couldn't go. So, Pastor added more people to the list. I would see a lot of preachers. Men, but no women. It would bother me, because I had this desire in my spirit. I used to question God, "Why do I have this feeling?" I was in a Baptist church where women were not allowed to preach God's Word, but God had told me that I would preach.

In 1991, it was prophesied to me that I was going to preach. I wondered how she knew this secret, because it was between God and me only. Who told her? God had to give me hope. I was at my last hope. At least I thought I was. I was growing up in a Baptist Church, hearing that women cannot preach. One day, back in the early 90's, when I was getting ready to go to church, I heard a woman preaching, and I stopped and looked at the TV. I loved to look at church programs on TV. The woman was Elder Debra B. Morton, of New Orleans. Her husband was Bishop Paul S. Morton. I asked myself, "Who gave her permission to preach? They said women cannot preach." I did not know that over twenty-five years from then, I would be preaching under this great woman of God, my Co-Pastor.

In 2004, with over thirty-seven years in leadership, God released me from one of the greatest Pastor I knew, the late Rev. O. Weems at Simpson Road Baptist Church. That was the hardest thing I ever had to do. I left my family, my friends, and my Godmother. I am here to tell someone who is reading this book, if God tells you to shift, please do. You will be okay. I am not saying that everything is going to be well. No; when I started my journey, the devil looked me in the face and said, "Welcome!" I looked the devil back in the face and said, "This is not what you want." I don't play with the devil. I learned that you cannot be on the battlefield for God, and not know how to stand. There have been plenty of times that the devil has tried to take me out. Sometimes, you might have to stand alone. You have to spend time with the Master, Jesus.

I want to encourage you to find a mountain, and make a date with the Master. He would love to come in and sit with you. Jesus said, in Revelations 3:20, *"Behold, I stand at the door, and knock: if any man hear My voice, and open the door, I will come in to him, and will sup with him, and he with Me."* If you stay with God, He will stay with you. Jesus will never leave you, nor forsake you. When the wicked comes upon you, believe that God has got you. Your enemies may want to kill your character. They want to take your name in vain, and say all kinds of things about you. I am here to tell you that I know what you are going through, and you will make it. I did.

The devil has nothing on you; stay with God. God knows who you are, and, "His eyes are on the sparrow, and I know He watches me and you. I sing because I am free, for His eye is on the sparrow, and I know He watches me."

I thank God that I know who I am. I am a changed woman. That spirit of sexual immorality that had me bound — that chain has been broken! I have been set free and delivered! I am on the waiting list for God to release me for that special person that can fulfill my every need. I know God is a Keeper. He has kept me from all diseases. We are living in a world where HIV is on a rampage, killing people, including those that are in the body of Christ. I pray that my testimony will touch the lives of others and break the yoke of the sexual immorality spirit. God's plan is for us to be in good health.

I am on the winning team! God has honored my request. My life passion is speaking, teaching, preaching, and prophesying God's word to His people. I pray that God will continue to use me to speak to His people through my writing. In December 2019, I will be releasing another book, *"How to Go Through Hell and Still Look Pretty."* This book will teach you how to face life changes and not look like what you have gone through. My prayer is that, in 2020, God will allow me to be a part of or establish a television program to teach and spread his word both locally and internationally. The Bible teaches me to write the vision and make it plain. *I Knew He had a Plan…!*

8
Know Your Haters

"Do not I hate them, O Lord, that hate thee? and am not I grieved with those that rise up against thee?
I hate them with perfect hatred: I count them mine enemies." Psalm 139:21-22

I have learned in this life, that people will hate you without cause. Jesus was teaching, in John 15:18-19, *"If the world hate you, ye know that it hated Me before it hated you. If ye were of the world, the world would love his own: but because ye are not of the world, but I have chosen you out of the world, therefore the world hateth you."*

In Psalm 139:21-22, David's hatred

for his enemies, came from his zeal for God. David regarded his enemies as God's enemies. So, his hatred was a desire for God's righteous justice, and not personal vengeance. It is alright to be angry at people who hate God. But we must remember that it is God who deals with them, not us. If we truly love God, then we will be deeply hurt if someone hates Him.

When I look back at my life and how I was treated when I was a young adult, I realize that is why I always kept to myself. I always treat people right. I don't just walk up and mess with anyone. If I have to deal with you, I do. But, if you are not my responsibility, I will leave you alone. What I do not understand, is why people will look at others and judge them by what they look like, what they eat, the way they dress, the way they talk, or whatever. Many times, women will look at me and judge me without knowing what I am going through or have been through. I have never had too many problems with men doing that. What people don't know about me is that I am shy. I have to admit that since I am older now, I am a lot better. Some of the things others have said about me were, "She thinks she is cute. She think she is all that. She thinks she knows everything." What they did not know is that I never thought I was smart or knew everything. I just kept to myself, because I did not want anyone to know that I barely made it out of high school, and that I learned how to read when I was in my late twenties.

 I still struggle with pronouncing some words. Well, we all do. I have heard smart people stumble over words. Nevertheless, what I learned is that I am not dumb or illiterate. Everything comes with time. God has allowed some intelligent people in my life, that have helped me along the way. When I was a little girl, I was robbed from being smart and intelligent. The man who hurt me left me in this dark world. But God gave it all back. So, no matter what people think of you, God is able to restore what you have lost. You see, that is why I used to isolate myself. By the way, I am a loner, not lonely. I can be alone and be okay. However, God changed that. He allowed me to take college courses, graduate from seminary, obtain many certifications in early education, and much more.

With God's help, I've had many people come up to me and say, "I used to think you thought you were all that. I just did not like you." Now, how crazy is that? Also, people have said, "When I learned to know you for myself, I loved you. You have a great heart and love God's people and treat people right. But, if someone messes with you, you know how to get them off you." There are some people who used to hate me, and now they are my friends for life.

There was a time when I had no money and nowhere to live. I would buy a ten-dollar pack of weave for my hair. I used to be a Fashion Fair and MAC lady. Now, I wear Walmart and Kroger makeup. I still do, to this day. I am okay with it. I wear older suits, because you never saw it, and you think it is new. I have given away clothes better than the ones I have kept. With all that, people still hated on me. I would say that if they only knew what I was going through, they would be praying for me. This is my testimony: I never…I mean I never… look like what I am going through. If people are waiting for that to happen, it will never happen.

I told my daughter, if I get to the point where I cannot take care of myself, she had better not let me lay there and look like a mess. When I get married, I am going to tell my husband the same thing. Just let me stay in the house, and don't let everybody come see me. That is why I wrote down the names of people very close to me, so they can come and see me. I am not worried about that, because God is my Keeper. He takes care of His own. I learned this from my father, when he became very ill. He did not let anybody come to see him. If you were not his children, you could not come see that man. He did not play with us. Until his death, I was his caregiver. I did whatever my dad said. You better believe it. I kept him clean and kept his house clean. You never smelled a "sick smell", when you came around him. I still battle with people hating on me, and trying to kill my gift from God. They are thinking that they can stop the gift that God has given me. They can never take me out. They will not take advantage of me. I know God sees them. He doesn't miss anything.

    I am not trying to be on anybody's platform. God knows that He called me. I am already struggling with some things, and I have no time for those people. If they laugh at me, you already know what I am going to do. God said, "I made you, and you are wonderfully made." Somebody is reading this book, thinking that they are not good enough. People have counted you out, left you for dead, and said you will never be somebody. But I am here to tell you what God told me. "I created you to praise Me, not man. This battle is not yours. It's Mine."

"And Moses said unto the Lord, O my Lord, I am not eloquent, neither heretofore, nor since Thou hast spoken unto thy servant: but I am slow of speech, and of a slow tongue. And the Lord said unto him, who hath made man's mouth? or who maketh the dumb, or deaf, or the seeing, or the blind? Have not I the Lord? Now therefore go, and I will be with thy mouth, and teach thee what thou shalt say."
Exodus 4:10-12

Moses pleaded with God to let him out of his mission. After all, he was not a good speaker and would probably embarrass both himself and God. God looked at Moses' problem quite differently. What Moses needed was help from God to direct him in what to say and how to do the right things. God made his mouth and would give him the words to speak. It is easy for us to focus on our weaknesses, but if God asks us to do something, then he will help us get the job done. If the job involves some of our weak areas, then we can trust that He will provide words, strength, courage, and ability where needed. Just know, that you belong to God, and He takes care of His own.

In Psalm 139:22 it says, *"I hate them with perfect hatred."* This is similar to saying, "I don't like you, but I love you." We all have hated someone or something. The dictionary says that a hater is a person who greatly dislikes a specified person or things. Hating is the result of being a hater. A hater is not exactly jealous. The hater does not really want to be the person he or she is hating. I hate when someone makes another person feel bad or unwanted. I hate when someone laughs at someone else who cannot help themselves. As Christians, we should not act like the world does. We have to realize that some people don't know who they are, and don't care about anyone one else, besides themselves. We have to love them anyway.

"Hold not thy peace, O God of my praise; For the mouth of the wicked and the mouth of the deceitful are opened against me: they have spoken against me with a lying tongue. They compassed me about also with words of hatred; and fought against me without a cause. For my love they are my adversaries: but I give myself unto prayer. And they have rewarded me evil for good, and hatred for my love." Psalm 109:1-5

David was angry at being attacked by evil people who slandered him and lied. Yet, David remained a friend and a man of prayer. While we must hate evil, and work to overcome it, we must love everyone, including those who do evil. God tells us to love them. We are called to hate the sin, but love the person.

"If a man say, I love God, and hateth his brother, he is a liar: for he that loveth not his brother whom he hath seen, how can he love God whom he hath not seen? And this commandment have we from Him, that he who loveth God loves his brother also." 1 John 4:20-21

We will always have haters around us. Keep your eyes on God. He will never let you down. The song that encourages my heart is, "I Come to The Garden Alone." I love the beautiful words of the song. *"I come to the garden alone, while the dew is still on the roses. And the voice I hear, falling on my ear, the Son of God discloses. And He walks with me, and He talks with me, and He tells me I am His own. And the joy we share as we tarry there, none other has ever known."*

9
A New Heart

*"Search me, O God, and know my heart:
try me, and know my thoughts:
And see if there be any wicked way in
me, and lead me in the way everlasting."
Psalm 139:23-24*

Growing up in my home church, the choir sang this song: "Search Me Lord". The words of the song say, "If you find anything in me not like You, take it out. I want to be right. I want to be whole." As long as I can remember, I have always tried to treat people right, because that is how I was raised. My father taught us to not mess with anybody, talk about other people, or laugh at people that have less than you. What I've come to realize, is that everybody was not teaching their children the same thing. Some children would laugh at other children, if they did not have what they had. I had a friend who would miss days from school, because she did not have very much. They laughed at me too, sometimes, because I did not have new clothes.

    I discovered, at an early age, that how you feel about people, and how you treat people, matters to God. As I have grown up, I believe that people have gotten worse. Sometimes I think, "Where has the love gone?" I pray that every believer would pray, and ask God to search our hearts, because we all are sinners living in a sinful world. I know that I have not always treated people right. I used to have some very funny ways. I would be talking and enjoying being around my friends, then sometimes I wanted to be alone. I often tell people that I love being alone. It doesn't bother me to be alone. I can travel and go out to dinner by myself.

I am okay, because being alone is different from being lonely.

Some people are lonely and very needy. They always need someone around them. It doesn't matter what and how people are, we have to treat people right. Let me tell you this: when I was dating, it was my way or no way. That is why I was by myself. I used to find myself being mean to people. I would look at them like they were crazy. I have left people feeling bad. I remember my mother telling me, "Latausher, nobody has to do anything for you. Nobody owes you nothing." My late Pastor used to always have us read 1 Corinthians 13. That talks about love and how God requires us to love one another. He often said, "You have gifts from God, but if you lack love, it is nothing to God."

It was difficult for me to understand why God called me to preach His Word to His people, when I did not like them like that. I did not want to be around people like that. I never thought that I did not need anybody. I just didn't want to be bothered. That is why I don't like asking people for anything, because some people think you have to be bothered with them. You know how people are, they will start to say, "She only calls or comes around when she wants something." Little did they know, if they needed something from me, they could just get it and go. The same went for me; just give it and move on. I know that I was raised to love, and I did when I fully understood.

> ***"When I was a child, I spake as a child, I understood as a child, I thought as a child: but when I became a man, I put away childish things."***
> ***1 Corinthians 13:11***

When I was thirty-five, my life changed. I really shifted. I started liking God's people, when I started preaching. I always treated people right. I've always hated to see people mistreat other people. I will always help people in need. I just didn't want to be bothered. I put away a lot of childish things. If you know me, you know that I fight to the end for the people I care about, especially if someone is weaker than the other person. I used to get on anybody who bothered my sisters and brothers, especially my sister, Vella. I love me some Vella. She always was my heart. They knew it too. She has gone on to be with Jesus, in that resting place.

If I was in a store and saw someone being mean to someone else, I would tell them how to treat people. I know, maybe it was none of my business, but I just cannot stand to see someone thinking that they can just treat people however they want to treat them. What gets to me the most, is watching church people mistreat one another. I can talk about them. That is where I am at the most- at church. When it happens at church, it makes it worse. Paul was talking about us, in Romans 1:21, when he said, *"Because that, when they knew God, they glorified Him not as God, neither were thankful; but became vain in their imaginations, and their foolish heart was darkened."* I found out that I was not better than them, if I was going to get upset and get back at people. Sometimes, I was not doing it out of love.

"The heart is deceitful above all things, and desperately wicked: who can know it?" Jeremiah 17:9

Please believe that I pray for a new heart every day. Well, some days I forget to ask. David asked God to search his heart and mind, and point out any wrong motives that may have been behind his strong words. David asked God to search for sin and point it out, even to the level of testing his thoughts. I pray that we make this verse our prayer. We must pray also for a new heart.

"Cast away from you all your transgressions, whereby ye have transgressed; and make you a new heart and a new spirit: for why will ye die, O house of Israel?

For I have no pleasure in the death of him that dieth, saith the Lord God: wherefore turn yourselves, and live ye."
Ezekiel 18:31-32

God wants us to have a changed heart. We have to allow Him to work in us. It is not something we can do for ourselves; the Holy Spirit does it. If we renounce our life direction of sin and rebellion, and turn to God, He will give us a new direction, a new love, and new power to change. You can begin by faith. Trust in God's power to change your heart and mind. When we allow God to change our hearts and minds, our lives change. People will see us in a new light. Old things are passed away, and God does not take pleasure in us dying in sin.

"And she shall bring forth a son, and thou shalt call his name Jesus: for he shall save his people from their sins."
Matthew 1:21

This means that the Lord saves! Jesus

came to earth to save us, because we cannot save ourselves from sin. Jesus did not come to help people save themselves. He came to be their Savior, and to deliver them from the power and the penalty of sin. That is why, if our heart is not right, God wants us to have a pure heart. If you don't have a pure heart, ask God to change your heart.

"Create in me a clean heart, O God; and renew a right spirit within me."
Psalm 51:10

Since we are born as a sinner, we must ask God to cleanse us from within, cleaning our hearts and spirit for new thoughts and desires. What is in our heart, matters to God. It shows God how we love, give, witness and serve His people. That is how people will know that we are saved. We are kingdom builders. We are building our lives for the kingdom. We must seek the least, the last, and the lost. Let God give you a new heart.

10
Conclusion

We have heard, in the church, and outside of the church as well, Jeremiah 29:11, *"For I know the thoughts that I think toward you, saith the Lord, thoughts of peace, and not of evil, to give you an expected end."* What I know, is that everybody can memorize this- the saved and the unsaved. This scripture will encourage you, no matter what your plans are. We are all encouraged by God, a Leader, who stirs us to move ahead. He believes that we can do the task that He has given us, and He will be with us, all the way. God is that kind of Leader. He knows what is best for us. Some people think, when God has a plan for their life, that going through challenges will not have to be part of His plan. We will have bad days. We will suffer. We will have many hardships. Who can say it better than Paul?

"Not that I speak in respect of want: for I have learned, in whatsoever state I am, therewith to be content."
Philippians 4:11

If anybody was going through something, it was Paul. His plan was to go to Rome. Now, between the time God gave him the plan to go, and when he went, he had never thought he was going to go through all that he went through. When I said yes to God, to preach His Word and to serve His people, I would never have thought my life would become a rollercoaster ride. I am up one minute and down the next minute. I had many dark days, but it was all in His plan. One thing I can say, is that God never left me, because I knew I was on an assignment for Jesus. I knew I had to go out to preach to a dying world. God put me in some place that I would have never went to on my own. I had to learn how to smile, when I wanted to cry; how to run, when I wanted to walk; how to be talked about, when I was not bothering anybody; how to fast, when I wanted to eat; how to live in a place I did not want to live in; how to stand on God's Word, when I wanted to give up; how to look at wrong, when I wanted to make it right. I learned that it was for God's glory. I learned that I will let nothing come between me and God, His Son Jesus, and my Helper, the Holy Spirit.

    In this life, traveling through this world, we will have some bumpy paths, but don't get off the path. Every person dreams and makes plans for their future. Some people make good plans, and some people make bad plans. Then they work hard to see those dreams and plans come true. I remember watching something on television. This man planned to rob a bank, while he was in prison. Now isn't that crazy for you to be in prison, and plan to rob a bank when you get out? Well, he robbed the bank. He got away with it, for a little while. Guess what; his plans did not go well. He got caught and went back to prison. He made wrong plans.

I know someone who told this lady that she will never preach. She could not understand it. If God said it, why not? Well, it took her years for it to come to pass. I am here to tell you; it came to pass. This means that I know the plans God has for me. Never discard your plans for anyone, if God put them in your spirit. Whatever your plans are, make sure you choose what is right and not wrong. If God has plans for your life, even the devil in hell can't do anything about it.

In Genesis, God had plans to save His people, and God will use anybody to make it happen. You might have to give up something or go through hell, like Joseph. Genesis 45:4-5, *"And Joseph said unto his brethren, Come near to me, I pray you. And*

Conclusion

they came near. And he said, I am Joseph your brother, whom ye sold into Egypt. Now therefore be not grieved, nor angry with yourselves, that ye sold me hither: for God did send me before you to preserve life."

Although Joseph's brothers had wanted to get rid of him, God used their evil actions to fulfill His plan. Yes, God wants to prosper you, but His greatest plan is for us to share Him with others. It is okay to live in the big house, drive the fine car, and go where we want. But our number one goal should be Christ-focused.

God promised us rest on earth. Joseph told his brothers that what they intended for harm, God intended for His good, to accomplish the saving of many lives. Joseph was rejected, kidnapped, enslaved, and imprisoned. Although his brothers had been unfaithful to him, he graciously forgave them and shared his prosperity. That is why we have to be careful how we treat people. The person who you cuss out, thinking that they are nobody, might just be the person that comes back and helps you.

To make the most of life, we must include God's plans, in our plans. He alone knows what is best for us. He alone can fulfill His purpose for us, as we make plans and dreams. God has done some great things in my life and still is doing them. This is my first book on my own. In the first book I wrote, I had the opportunity to share my testimony with many other women around the world, on relationships. I can tell you this: the best is yet to come. I had to make it, to save a generation.

About the Author

Latausher L. Fletcher is an Atlanta, Georgia native, who is fondly referred to as "The Preacher Woman from the South." She is the Founder of "I'm Thirsty Women's Fellowship," which has been changing and transforming lives, for more than sixteen years. She is a graduate of B.J. Holland Institution of Ministry, as well as Hick and Hick Institution. Latausher is the proud mother of four children.

P.O. Box 453
Powder Springs, Georgia 30127

www.entegritypublishing.com
info@entegritypublishing.com

770.727.6517

www.ingramcontent.com/pod-product-compliance
Lightning Source LLC
Chambersburg PA
CBHW052106070526
44584CB00017B/2351